Knocking the Door of Happiness

Anuradha.H.N

Astha Shukla

ISBN: 9789390261734
First Published in 2020

Walnut Publication (Vyusta Ventures LLP)
#722, Esplanade One, Rasulgarh,
Bhubaneswar – 751010, India

Preface

For a long time, we have been observing changes in our lifestyles, working patterns, our preferences in movies & sports, but one thing has been constant - **'the struggle to stay happy'**.

The main reason for writing this book is to bring happiness in the life of an individual.

A lot has been said and written about physical and mental health but how this co-relates to your inner peace and happiness is something which has a wider scope for research and discussions.

We have tried to analyse the approach of being happy from a different perspective which includes Spiritual, Psychological and other aspects of one's life.

We strongly believe that one's source of happiness differs from the other individual but in the end, everyone wants to have a peaceful sleep & a happy morning.

As quoted by 'Eleanor Roosevelt-

"Happiness is not a goal, it is a by-product".

We have tried to analyse and interpret the outcomes of our day to day activities and all the little achievements (which we usually tend to ignore) plays an important part to lead a happy life.

This book does not talk about any thumb rule as the title itself - 'Knocking the door of Happiness' is very subjective, we have tried to showcase few aspects which can co-relate with individuals of all the age groups. They can surely take few best practices to implement in their daily lives which will help them to appreciate all the little things and to acknowledge the happiness lies within.

Acknowledgment

We feel immensely blessed to have an opportunity to write this book.

As researchers, we have been keenly studying the sample response towards the basic problem and tried to apply the same concept while writing this book.

We would like to show our deepest gratitude towards our experts who have been able to spare their time irrespective of their busy schedule to contribute towards the successful completion of this book.

We would like to thank our family members for their endless love & enormous support.

We are so blessed by the universe to inculcate the thought of writing the book.

We would like to thank Dr. M R Ranganatha (Chairman SMART Academy) who have been our mentor and guide throughout the journey and being one of our most valuable experts and support system who made sure that we do not deviate from our aim.

We would also like to thank Ms. Smita Kumari, Mr. Siddharth Chandrashekhar, Ms. Janine Thwaites, Mr. Ashish Chandarana, Mrs. Anupama Chandra and Mr. Rohit Singh who were the best people to guide us and to be the part of our expert panel.

A big thank you to Aditya Dakhle who have been a constant support by helping us over all the social media and designing part.

And all this would just have been a dream without the support of the team 'Walnut Publication'.

To everyone who has been there with us and to everyone we may meet via this book we thank you all.

Our Expert

Dr. M R Ranganatha
Chairman- SMART Academy

Ms. Smita Kumari

Clinical Psychologist in District Disability Rehabilitation Centre under Social Justice and Disability Welfare Dept. Govt. of MP (Vidisha)

Rehabilitation Psychologist and Special Educator in Learning Disability (RCI)

Mr. Siddharth Chandrashekhar
Counsel, Bombay High Court
B. A. LL. M. (UK)

Ms. Janine Thwaites

Motivational Speaker & Writer (UK)

(Pen Name: Lord Writing)

Mr. Rohit Singh
Expert Analyst at
ETC management services India Pvt Ltd

Mrs. Anupama Chandra

Currently Working as 'Independent
Communication Consultant for PR Agencies'

Is a Counsellor and was a 'Crime Reporter'.

Mr. Ashish Chandarana

Management and Quality Expert

Contents

Introduction

Knocking the Door of Happiness?

Wow right!

Who doesn't wants to be happy in this world?

Everyone wants to be happy but, happiness and the reasons for being happy differs from one person to another.

In today's life, maintaining mental health and inner strength is very much necessary.

Learning the art of improving your inner strength leads us to a peaceful mind and happiness.

Emotional health can lead to success in work, relationships, and health. In the past, researchers believed that success made people happy. New research reveals that it's the other way around. Happy people are more likely to work towards their goals, find the resources they need, and attract others with their energy and optimism — key building blocks of success according to APA.

"Happiness is a journey, not a destination"-The Monk who sold his Ferrari by Robin Sharma.

We often search for happiness in places and people we come across, how far things will stay is always questionable. We have been taught and raised in a way that we end up considering material aspects that brings us happiness.

Often, as a kid, most of us were told to study hard get good marks to lead a happy & successful life in the future, but is it a thing that matters?

Our education system also teaches only those subjects, which directs us towards materialistic needs (earning). We are raised in a manner where by getting good marks we eventually end up getting a good or satisfactory and sustainable job. But we need to have good mental health and to stay happy it is very much important. However, we don't realise all this soon, due to the way we were made to see the world.

The authors believe that true happiness has a different meaning which differs from individual to individual. One might feel the happiness by scoring the highest marks or by purchasing a costly vehicle.

On contrary to this someone else might feel an immense level of happiness just by feeding a stray animal or by sipping tea or coffee after a tiring day.

Do you observe, how hard it is to quantify the level or degree of happiness!

There are instances, we have gloomy days and some days are just happy days. Your reason/s for being happy differs from age to age & sometimes it differs based on your sexual orientation too.

It is not wrong to say that happiness or the feeling which makes you happy has a strong impact on your emotions too.

Many studies have revealed that when you are happy and positive you attract a lot more positivity as compared to your gloomy phase.

As a reader, most of us get influenced by the writers, likewise the quote "we have started our introduction", has an impact on us.

One cannot stay happy throughout for just one reason but you keep finding happiness in all the little things in and around you.

Many have written about & talked about 'Happiness' and we are trying to do the same with a different approach. We are trying to come up with how different aspects of happiness in one's life may or may not have just a spiritual or psychological approach but it does have an impact on certain aspects of our lives.

Remember, no one can make you happy until & unless you want to feel it in your way where you have your definition or meaning to the word 'Happiness'. We are here to guide you and walk you through the path on how can you identify where your mental peace and happiness lies.

We have interacted with some of our experts' working as Psychologists, Lawyers, Educationist, etc. and we have tried to share their approach towards life and happiness which will open the doors of happiness for you which seem closed or locked for a while.

Happiness is not in what we have, but all about how we think.

"Happiness lies within the self".

We can guide you towards the road that can lead you towards a happy life.

Chapter 1

What is Happiness?

We believe this is one topic that is highly subjective and will always have a scope for discussion. So, when we say it's subjective we are letting you have your own believes associated with this one term 'Happiness' and describe it in your convenient way as there is no thumb rule to define it.

As an individual, I must have been happy when I have achieved the highest marks as a student or got appreciated at work by my supervisor. The term will hold a different meaning for me at every stage of my life, at different age group my meaning and understanding towards this term will differ.

This is not just about me but all of us because we all go through different phases in our lives and we all experience a new situation almost every day until the day we depart.

So, what are we looking at?

What are we trying to explain when we ask- What is happiness?

Well, we aren't trying to teach any rocket science here. However, most of the things we may discuss further will sound familiar to you as you must have heard and felt it at some or the other part your lives.

This one-term happiness is used in the context of mental or rather emotional states, inclusive of pleasant or positive emotions ranging from contentment to immense joy. It is also used in the context of life satisfaction, emotional well-being, and eudemonic. Since 1960, research has been conducted over this topic, in a wide variety of scientific disciplines including:
– Gerontology
– Social Psychology and Positive Psychology
– Clinical and Medical Research, and
– Happiness Economics.

The United Nations Sustainable Development Solutions Networks publish the annual Happiness Index across the globe in its journal. Amazingly, this concept was first coined in 1979 by the King of Bhutan, 'Jigme Singye Wangchuck' who said-

"We do not believe in the Gross National Product. Gross National Happiness is very important".
And since then, the economist started prioritizing happiness over other factors like wealth, comfort, or economic growth.

While we proceed further we want you to understand or to know how different religious believes have tried to explain the term happiness. In **Buddhism**, happiness forms a central theme. It is believed that one achieves happiness only by removing the cravings or desires in all forms. More mundane forms of happiness, such as acquiring wealth and maintaining good friendship are also recognized as worthy goals for people.

Buddhism also encourages the generation of loving-kindness and compassion the desire for the happiness and welfare of all spirits.

Hinduism focuses on Advaita Vedanta, the ultimate goal of life is happening in the sense the duality between Atman and Brahman is transcended and one realizes oneself to be the 'self' in all.

In Yoga Sutra, Patanjali (author) wrote quite exhaustively on the psychological and ontological roots of bliss.

Happiness in **Judaism** or **Simcha (Hebrew)** is considered as an important element towards the service of God.

The primary meaning of 'happiness' in various European languages involves good fortune, chance or happening.

The meaning in Greek philosophy, however, refers primarily to ethics.

In Catholicism, the ultimate end of human existence consists of infelicity.

Al-Ghazali, a Persian theologian philosopher and prolific Sunni Muslim author has written-

"The Alchemy of Happiness (Kimiya-Yi Saadat) which emphasized the importance of observing the ritual requirements of Islam, the actions that would lead to salvation and avoidance of sin.

Each religion and culture has described their own version of happiness and the paths to achieve them.

Through all this, we did observe that this is a very subjective term which can be changed according to one's own version of reality, belief and religious preaching/followings.

It's a wide topic when we talk about the religious aspect of the term, so we have tried to focus our whole study towards 'Spirituality and Psychology'.

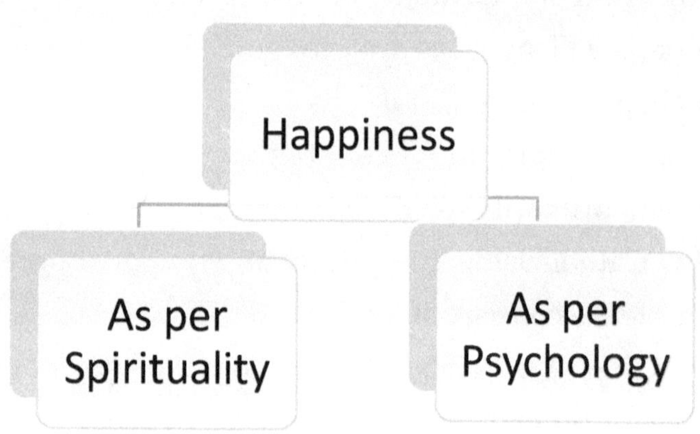

To understand what happiness means as per spirituality and psychology we must know what the two terms exactly mean...

• **As per Spirituality**: In Sanskrit, 'spirituality' is known as *Adhyaatma*, derived from two words 'Adhi' meaning about the topic and 'Atma' means the soul. The soul is the god principle within us and is our true nature. It is the main component of the subtle body, which is a fractional part of the supreme god principle. Its characteristics are absolute truth (Sat), absolute consciousness (Chit) and Bliss (Anand). The soul is unaffected by the ups and downs (commonly known as happiness and unhappiness) one's experiences in life as it is perpetually in a blissful state.

"Spirituality, thus deals with understanding the nature of the soul and one's journey back to identifying its true purpose. Spirituality is an expansive science about how to be blissful.

- **As Per Psychology**: In 1884 James Surly defined psychology as the science of the 'inner world' as distinct from physical science which study the physical phenomena.

It can be defined as the studies of mental process and behavior which is commonly talked as 'Mental Well-Being now. The term psychology comes from the Greek word *'psyche'* meaning 'Breath, Spirit, Soul' and the word *'logic'* meaning 'study of'.

In 1892 Wilhelm Wundt defined psychology as the science which studies the internal experiences. These psychologists gave up the metaphysical concept of mind as a spiritual substance. Psychology is behavior science and deals with experience and behavioral aspect of an individual.

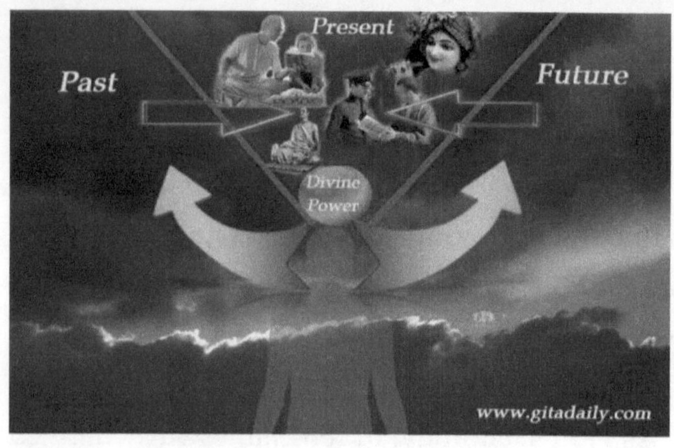

Happiness - Spiritual Aspect

Many studies have been executed and many are still undergoing to establish the relationship between happiness and religion, spirituality, money etc.

Ed Diener and his son Robert Biswas Diener published a book called "Happiness-Unlocking the mysteries of psychological wealth" where they tried to review as much literature to identify if religion keeps a person happy…
The study revealed that many religious people tend to be happy but it may not be the case across all the nations due to diversity and faith. The religion majorly encourages us to live life selflessly with positive emotions such as compassion, gratitude and forgiveness. But this message provided by the religion can also be regarded by those who are agnostic and atheistic. A further study which was conducted by psychologist Mark Holder and Colleagues at the University of British Columbia in Canada (published in 2008), where the children under the age group of 9-12 were undertaken to study the emphasize on youth being more religious or

spiritual and the link between spirituality and meaning, hope, positive social norms and social networks.

The results were inclined towards spirituality than the religion.

The study concluded that children or young people who feel that their lives have meaning and value and who develop deep quality relationship are happier than those who don't.

However, this also disapproves the previous believes that well-behaved children are religious, and factors like private or government schools being religious may not play a significant role in their lives.

A research project by Dr. Michael Yi and Sian Cetton at the University of Cincinnati revealed links between spirituality and happiness among teenagers.

A study was conducted with a sample size of 155 adolescents where the researchers compared teenagers with 'Inflammatory Bowel Disease (IBD) with their healthy peers.

The analysis showed that while spirituality helped all the young cope with life's challenges but it was especially helpful for the ones with IBD.

Also, the higher level of spiritual well-being was associated with the fewer depressive symptoms and better emotional well-being among the teenagers/adolescents.

It has been observed that many believe spirituality and religion are the same, but to lay down the very difference between the two is very important.

Religion often tends to be sectarian. A 'sect' is a group of people who usually think that their 'path to god' is the best and the preferable one (if not the only one).

Whereas, spirituality is to work on the fundamental principles of 'as many paths to god as there are people'. Just like a doctor does not advice the same medicine for different ailments for different patients, similarly the same type of spiritual practice does not necessarily benefit everyone.

Irrespective of who we are and where we come from, our need to experience happiness in our lives drives all our worldly pursuits. This need is common to all of us regardless of cultural background, religion, gender, social or financial status etc.

Spiritual research was conducted and it was found that on an average people experience happiness only 30% of the time.

The main reason we experience unhappiness is due to a problem in our lives both physical and mental or psychological cause. However, many of us are unaware that their physical or psychological problem can have a spiritual root cause too; which means that even if though a problem is primarily due to spiritual reasons, it can manifest as a physical and psychological problem.

We all go through different phases in our lives and at some point, many of us wonder-
"Why do I exist?" or "What is the sole purpose of my life?"
'Was it all about studies (marks), getting a job, getting married, buying the car/house, to get recognized at work and ultimately we die...'
According to the Science of Spirituality, there are only two reasons for being born:

1. The very first purpose of life is to complete one's destiny or Karma that one is born with.

2. The second and most important purpose of life is to grow spiritually.

Practicing spirituality helps us with both these purposes. It helps to overcome adverse fortune that drives us to unhappiness and it also helps us to grow spiritually.

There are many ways one can follow spirituality and can discipline his/her life by following a few practices

1. **Begin and end your day with a moment of reflection:** This could be considered as that time you devote yourself for prayer or meditation. Where you focus on the divine and focus on your breath to ground yourself in preparation for your daily duties.

2. **Find a muse or an inspiration:** From spending time with your pet to listening to music, drawing, dancing or having a conversation with like-minded people to reading books which helps you to stay positive and inspire you to do things which enrich your experience and provide encouragement for your spiritual pursuits.

3. **Self-acceptance and compassion towards others:** Do not let the factors like colour, age, gender define you. Love yourself for who you are and clear the paths where you doubt yourself. Do not degrade yourself, always remember- "You are enough and you are selected to play this role. No-one else could have performed it better than you." Work towards self-elevation and love yourself a little more with each passing day. When we talk about self-acceptance and self-love we don't want you to think of acting selfishly towards others. The world needs them just like the way it needs you. Treat them with love and accept them for all that they are. It's easy to find someone to lean on when you are in trouble, be there for others when they need you. Empathize when they are troubled the world do not need sympathy. They need love and affection as much as you do there is a thin line of difference between the two. Most of the times we know the solutions but we need someone to speak with so learn to 'Empathize'.

4. **Letting Go:** Accept the change and move ahead to a new venture of your life. We pursue

our primary education get promoted to middle and then to higher education, we lose friends, some of our favorite teachers, moving from one city to another for a better career and opportunities we keep on moving, so why don't we let go of our past? There are times we all make mistakes but we can only see them as building blocks in our lives and learn a lesson to be a better person. Carrying the burden from the past and evaluating all the things based on it will do no good to anyone. Remember, when we say evaluating we do not want you to ignore the factor 'what could go wrong' but anticipate and to take that leap of faith to move ahead. Sometimes, it takes time to get over the past but one needs to because you cannot be in kindergarten for the rest of your life.

The more you follow the spiritual path the more you will have time to introspect and to analyze. This will help you to clear the chaos in your mind and act unbiased towards others.

The less you judge people and things the more self-satisfied you feel, which eventually leads you towards happiness in life.

Happiness: Psychological Aspect

Many studies have been conducted and over the last three decades (Diener, 2013) with one most basic question that happiness investigators routinely examine is-

"How happy are people in general?"

Some psychologists have suggested that happiness consists of three distinct elements-

1. The pleasant life – enjoying daily pleasure,
2. The good life- using skills for enrichment,
3. Meaningful life- contributing to the greater good.

A precise definition of happiness might incorporate each of these elements: an enduring state of mind consisting of joy, contentment and other positive emotions and the sense that one's life has a meaning and value (Lyubomirsky, 2001)

"Happiness is a mystery like religion and should never be rationalized" – G.K Chesterton (English Author 1874-1936)

It is not wrong to say many studies have identified that one can be extremely happy for one reason but that can surely not be considered as the sole reason for happiness.

It has been and it will be a very subjective experience. What brings elation to one person will not necessarily satisfy another but from a psychological viewpoint, we must be able to quantify this state of mind to understand it.

"The happiness of your life depends upon the quality of your thoughts" Marcus Aurelius

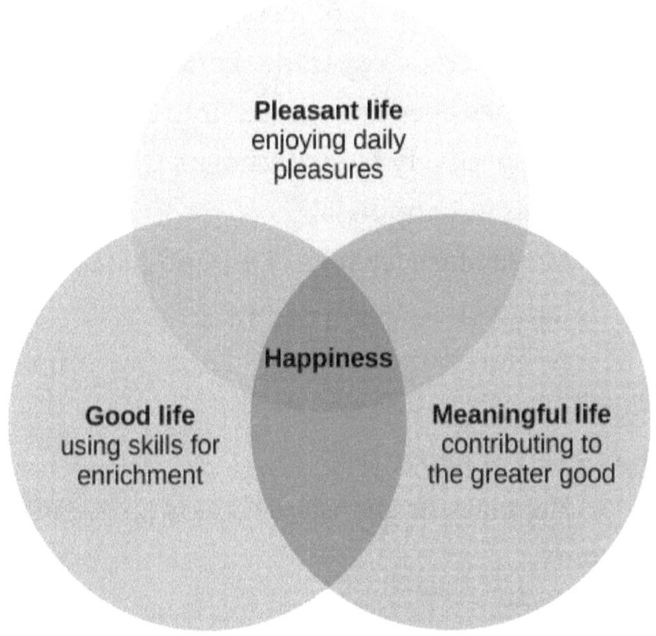

Source: https://courses.lumenlearning.com/wsu-sandbox/chapter/the-pursuit-of-happiness/

Most people want to be happy (inner happiness). Some have lost the will to live, but the majority of human beings are engaged—consciously or unconsciously—in actions designed to improve their levels of happiness.

Sometimes, these actions can have the opposite effect, or can make us happy in the short term but unhappy in the longer term. This is why there are many definitions of happiness, and the concept has evolved so much over the centuries.

Happiness has been categorized into 3-levels and 4-levels respectively by few scholars.

Three levels of happiness

- Momentary feelings of joy and pleasure
- Judgments about feelings
- A higher meaning of life, being content with what you have.

Four levels of happiness

- Happiness from material objects (materialistic pleasure)
- Happiness from comparison: working towards the betterment of self.
- Happiness from being kind & generous towards others and making the world a better place to live.

- Ultimate or perfect happiness - finding your calling

Happiness can be described as very different things:

- Short-term: your current feelings and emotions, such as pleasure, joy, or sadness. This is what you experience here and now.

- Medium-term: your subjective life satisfaction. In a study about how happiness differs across cultures, it was described as the "overall appreciation of one's life as-a-whole" (by Ruut Veenhoven).

- Long-term: your conscious approach to flourishing as a human being. Aristotle called it a life of "virtuous activity per reason."

The first two are probably very familiar to you, so let us talk about the third vision of happiness—the long-term one—. Aristotle coined it Eudemonia in Greek, which is sometimes translated as **"human flourishing"**.

The reason behind such a philosophy (logos in Greek) is unique to human beings, the ideal goal of human life is the fullest exercise of one's reason or we may just say it as one's purpose.

It is not enough to be skilled or talented to live a good life. To achieve happiness, we must be engaged in intellectual stimulating activities.

But one must not ignore other important dimensions such as friends, wealth, and power (which is also a very important aspect of many modern psychologists). It is highly doubtful that we could achieve Eudemonia if we were completely missing one of these crucial aspects (human beings are social animals and we need human relations).

In layman's terms, it's hard to be happy if you're broke and without any friends or people whom you can count on. And, as we have mentioned how psychologists have accepted these factors the same has been discussed in one of the most known theories of happiness in psychology, the pyramid of Maslow.

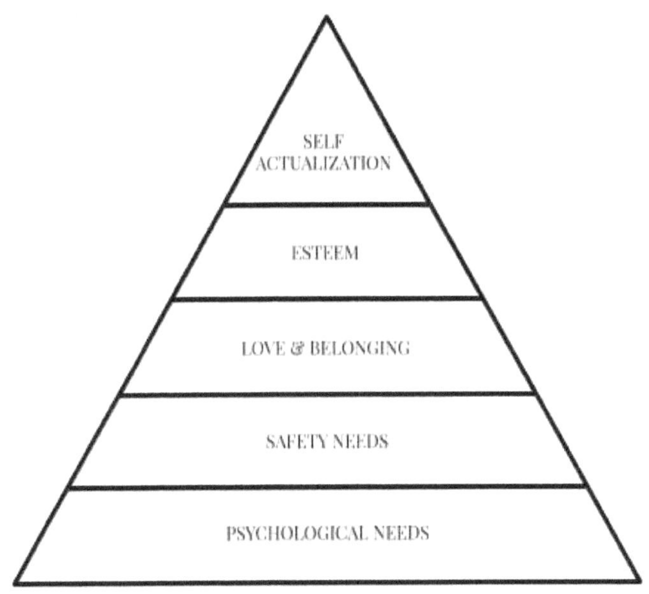

Source: https://nesslabs.com/psychology-of-happiness

Theories of happiness in Psychology

Quantifying or measuring happiness is hard as we keep debating if happiness is objective or subjective? Is it about how your current feeling or in general? Is it pragmatic, or emotional?

Many writers and scholars are still debating to justify this and to draw the attention towards how important this field of research is, there is even a dedicated Journal of Happiness Studies.

But there are three main theories towards which many researchers are gravitating:

1. The Freedom of Choice Theory: The study conducted by Ronald Inglehart, a professor and scientist, the extent to which a society allows free choice/s has a major impact on one's happiness. When their basic needs are met, the level of happiness shows positive growth and this also depends on how much free choice people have it could be anything related to their career choices to the freedom of learning a new skill-sets or choosing their peer or friends.

2. The Self-Determination Theory: Studies have revealed that the ability to make choices without external influence or external interference is also an important factor to live a happy life. The zeal and willingness to grow by staying focused can determine the level of happiness in one's life.

3. The Positive Psychology Theory: The third and highly discussed psychology theory discussed lately is the positive psychology which considers that instead of trying to fix things when they get broken, we should spend more time and energy improving our mental well being more positively and proactively.

There are times that fail to fulfill extremely high expectations leaving you depressed and unmotivated. Many studies have revealed that happiness is under-valued in Eastern cultures than Western ones.

Dr Carol Diane Ryff, an American academic and psychologist, has been studying psychological well-being and psychological resilience for decades. She created the Six-factor Model of Psychological Well-being, a theory that outlines the key factors to our happiness which is something we all do follow knowingly or unknowingly.

1. **Self-acceptance**: This focuses on acknowledging and accepting all aspects of yourself, the good and the bad. It's being aware of your strengths and weaknesses and trying to be realistic and rational in the way you assess your skills and talents. As they say, it is very important to accept yourself than seeking acceptance from the world.

2. **Autonomy**: Being independent in the way you think, and having confidence in your opinions irrespective of the social pressures. It indicates that you are free to make your own choices which also helps you to be self-confident.

3. **Environmental mastery**: This means you are feeling in charge or responsible. You take accountability for your actions and can use opportunities as they arise to address your personal needs. You can manage external factors and activities in your day-to-day life. It comes with a feeling of being in control of the situation in which you live, this could be closely related to the 'Work-Life Balance' we all have been talking about.

4. **Personal growth**: Personal growth is the effort towards one's continuous improvement through new experiences and constantly trying to become a better version of yourself.

5. **Positive relations with others**: Friends, family, colleagues—it's very important to have a meaningful relationship with others which include reciprocal empathy, affection, and various levels of intimacy. We being social and rational animals, need to build a good relation with the society, not just to gain respect or acquire some position, but also a sense of belonging and socialization.

6. **Purpose in life**: This one is a prime factor, finding meaning is about pursuing goals you deeply care about and creating value in your life. For some people, this can be achieved through religion, but you can find your purpose in life through meaningful work, philosophy, or even human connections.

Positive Psychology:

The positive psychology movement was introduced by Martin E.P. Seligman, Ph.D., former APA President, which focuses on enhancing or working towards what's good in life rather than fixing what's wrong or broken. The study considered twenty traits as personality characteristics that can be the "roots of a positive life," including the capacity to love and be loved, altruism, spirituality, creativity, courage, and wisdom. Researchers are studying the types of experiences that make people feel good, the personal traits that create happiness, and ways to create positive institutions.

The motive for the movement is to develop positive psychology techniques for all people.

Just like all other psychologist and the experts we have interacted the study revealed that money, drugs, and shopping are not the only factors which can help us attain happiness.

Positive psychology research is focused on what makes people happy. As we have mentioned earlier we tend to ignore all the little things in our day to day lives the recent studies have also found that happiness comes in every day as a simple reward. In a research conducted by Alice Isen, Ph.D., a professor in the psychology department of Cornell's Arts College, found that people experience a thrill when they get a free sample, find a quarter on the street or receive an unexpected gift--and the emotion associated to them makes it feel more generous, friendlier and healthier.

The emphasis on little things associated with our day to day lives plays an important role in triggering the positive emotions and impacting our behavior which is what positive psychology all about.

The Role of Positive Emotions in Positive Psychology

The purpose of positive psychology is to understand and foster the factors that allow individuals, communities, and societies to flourish (Seligman & Csikszentmihalyi, 2000).

Positive emotions serve as a building block or foundation towards optimal well-being. Certainly, moments in one's lives characterized by experiences of positive emotions such as joy, contentment, and love are the moments in which are not spoilt by the negative emotions like anxiety, sadness, anger, and despair. The overall balance of people's positive and negative emotions which is often termed as emotional stability has been considered to predict their judgments of subjective well-being. Kahneman (1999) stated that "objective happiness" can best be measured by tracing and further aggregating people's momentary experiences of good and bad feelings.

According to these perspectives, positive emotions signal growth. They not only flourish positive emotions in the present, but also pleasant moment for the long term as well. The take-home message is that positive emotions are worth nourishing, not just as end states in themselves but also as a way to achieve psychological growth and improved well-being over time.

Perspective on Emotions and Effect:

Working definitions of emotions and it's affect differs across researchers. Yet despite ongoing debate (e.g., Diener, 1999; Ekman & Davidson, 1994), a consensus is emerging that emotions are nothing but a subset of the wider aspect of affective phenomena. Emotions, according to this assumption, are best conceptualized as multi-component response tendencies that unfold over a comparatively short duration. Typically, an emotion begins with an individual's assessment of the self-belief of some antecedent event. This appraisal process may be either conscious or unconscious, and it stimulates a cascade of response pattern manifest across loosely associated component systems, such as self (biased) experience, facial expression, cognitive processing, and physiological changes.

Affect, in a general concept, refers to consciously triggered feelings. Although affect is present within emotions (as the component of self-experience), it is also present within many other affective factors, including physical sensations, attitudes, moods, and even traits. However, emotions are distinct from affect in multiple ways, as emotions are typically about some personally meaningful circumstance (i.e., they have a specific objective), whereas affect is often random or objectless. Also, emotions are often categorized as per emotion families, like fear, anger, joy, and love. On contrary Affect, is often conceptualized as varying along with two elements, either pleasantness or activation.

Perspectives on the Functions of Affect and Emotions:

Experiences of positive affect prompt individuals to engage with their environments and to participate in activities, many of which are adaptive for the individual. This association between positive affect and activity engagement justifies often-observed and recorded positivity offset or the frequency for individuals to experience mild positive effect, even in general contexts. Without such an offset, individuals would be less motivated to feel connected with their environments. Yet with such an offset, individuals showcase the adaptive bias to approach and explore new objects, people, and circumstances.

Since positive emotions include an element of positive affect, they too act as internal signals to approach or to continue. Also, positive emotions share this function with other positive affective states. Sensory pleasure, for instance, motivates people to approach and continue pursuing whatever stimulus is biologically necessary for them at the moment. Likewise, free-floating positive moods motivate people to continue any line of thinking or action that they have started. Though, the functioning of positive emotions that emphasize inclination towards or to continue may only capture the lowest common denominator across all affective states that share a pleasant subjective feel, leaving additional functions unique to specific positive emotions unexplored. Discrete emotion theorists often associate the function of specific emotions to the concept of specific action tendencies (Frijda, 1986; Frijda, Kuipers, & Schure, 1989; Lazarus, 1991; Levenson, 1994; Oatley & Jenkins, 1996; Tooby & Cosmides, 1990). Fear, for example, is associated with a desire to escape, anger with the desire to hurt, or to attack. It is not that people invariably act out these behaviors or desires when experiencing particular emotions. A key assumption from this perspective is that a specific action tendency is what makes an emotion more adaptive. These are among the actions that presumably worked best in helping humans survive when we talk about survival of the fittest. Another key idea from tire specific emotions perspective is that specific action tendency and physiological changes go hand in hand. So, for instance, when someone craves an urge to escape when in fear, that person's body reacts by mobilizing suitable autonomic support for the possibility of escaping or running away.

Although specific action habits have the urge to explain the function of certain positive emotions as well, the action tendencies identified for positive emotions are probably vague and unspecified or unclear. They resemble generic desires to do anything or do nothing more than urges to do something quite specific and meaningful, like flee, attack, or spit. And, if the action tendencies instigated by positive emotions are vague, their impact on survival may be inconsequential.

Happiness: Role of Dopamine and Serotonin on Mood and Negative Emotions:

A study conducted by Elena Baixauli (Department of Psychology, University of Valencia, Spain) talks about the scientific or neurological aspects where the hormones in a human body impact psychology and these are also known as Happy Hormones.

From a neurological point of view, there are hormones in our brain associated with positive emotions. Dopamine hormone is associated with happiness and serotonin regulates our mood.

When a person is physically attracted to someone, activation of dopamine, serotonin increased and the production of oxytocin, a hormone that reduces pain perception and increases the emotional bond we have with the other occurs, disconnecting the amygdale , a small neuron structure in the anterior part of the cerebrum , the part of the brain that is active against negative emotions like fear.

A study published in Psychological Science in 2008 identified that certain inherited genes are likely to account for 50 per cent of our happiness. But even if you're more down than up, you can make choices that will help you experience a brighter, happier life.

The D.O.S.E. Hormones:

- **D = Dopamine** is "Associated with love, enjoyment, motivation, and more, dopamine beckoning plays a central role in the brain's reward system. It is also critical for processes such as motor control, learning, and memory."

- **O = Oxytocin** is a hormone secreted by the posterior lobe of the pituitary gland, a pea-sized structure at the base of the brain. It's sometimes referred to as the "snuggle hormone" or the "love hormone".

- **S = "Serotonin** is called as the "don't worry, be happy" calming neurotransmitter. It plays multiple roles in the brain's biochemistry and is a critical component in facilitating sustained and deep sleep, maintaining a balanced mood, self-confidence, social engagement, and a healthy appetite. Additionally, it helps decrease our worries and concerns and is associated with learning and memory." Daniel G. Amen, MD

- **E = Endorphins** are chemicals produced naturally by the nervous system to cope with pain or stress. They are often referred to as the "feel-good" chemicals because they can act as a pain reliever and happiness booster.

Apart from the above mentioned D.O.S.E, there is another hormone which is Progesterone which helps you to sleep well and prevents anxiety, irritability, and mood swings. The volume of happy hormones drops as women enter per perimenopause after the age of 45-50, and this can be accelerated by excess stress and unhealthy foods. Experts such as Dr. Sara Gottfried, author of The Hormone Cure, say taking care of yourself (physically and mentally) and eating right is your first defense for balancing hormones.

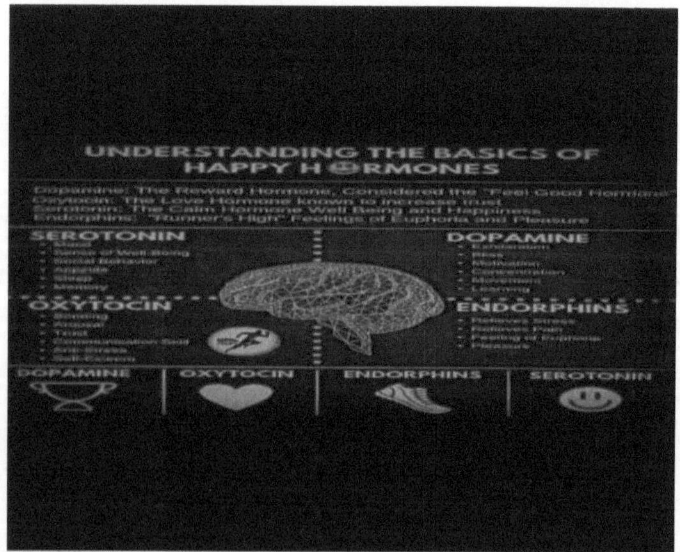

Natural ways to boost your happy hormones

Music: Listening to music is an amazing way to generate dopamine. In a 2011 study published in Nature Neuroscience, McGill University researchers reported that listening to music you love increases the level of feel-good dopamine. As they say, if you are feeling low, switch on to some good tunes. Eat carbs as they increase serotonin levels, which partly justifies why we crave sweet, starchy foods when we are feeling low. To light up your mood with the least negative impact, opt healthy, high-fiber sources of carbs such as dense whole-grain bread or quinoa.

Spend time with loved ones: Increase the level of oxytocin by doing pleasurable things such as spending time cuddling with your partner, your kids, or your pet(s), rather than spending time on social media.

Stress relievers: Increase estrogen with stress-relieving activities such as yoga, meditation, taking a hot shower, or whatever works for you. Plus, keep progesterone at optimum levels by eating well and avoiding saturated fat and sugar, and avoiding stress. And while you're at it, read up on the best ways to remind yourself that you're worthy of happiness.

There are many other ways one can work on their 'Happy Hormones' by doing things which give them immense pleasure like spending time with your pet, reading, cooking, writing, dancing, playing your favorite sports, etc.

The more we try to figure out the psychological aspect the more it makes sense as to how all the little things we tend to ignore on daily basis actually plays a vital role in our lives and how much impact it has on your mood and psychology.

Chapter 2

How is Happiness Different for Men and Women

We all crave for materialistic and non-materialist pleasure which may or may not contribute towards the long term happiness we seek for but it surely contributes towards the real-time or short-term happiness.

Men and women are different in a lot many ways and certainly, gender plays an important role in describing what gives happiness to a man or to a woman. What makes a man happy may not be the major factor a woman may consider which eventually leads towards her subjective definition of happiness.

A man may feel overwhelmed and delighted after a heavy workout session. Whereas, a woman may be extremely happy when she bakes the cake for the first time or just had a relaxing weekend after a tiresome or hectic week at work.

Many studies have been conducted and proved that a lot of men prefer playing video games when they are stressed and women prefer going out for shopping.

Studies try to establish a correlation between happiness and gender. Few suggested that happiness is related to achieving goals; women focus majorly on relationships and family life while men are more inclined towards financial and professional success.

Although various researches has reported that women and men are similar in most psychological traits, however, due to societal assumptions they are considered different and expected to occupy different roles. Customary theories state differences in gender roles were normal and healthy. Studies about the differences between women and men well-being have not generated consistent outcomes. It has also been found in different cultures that women scored lower than men in self-acceptance and autonomy. Many studies tried to scan out if the profession of men and woman are also the reason behind the different perspective towards seeking happiness and psychological well-being or is it just the societal assumptions.

When it comes to men, women, and happiness, then it is not enough to talk about what makes each gender happy as separate entities; we also need to consider what makes them happy together as companions or partners. Men and women operate as individuals, but they also operate as companions when in an intimate relationship. While personality type and attitude certainly influence happiness and the things that make them happy, it's impossible to overlook the cultural norms that differentiate what men and women should or could aspire to do.

It is also important to differentiate between the two types of happiness that psychology defines: Hedonic and Eudaimonia Happiness.

Researchers define the pleasure that is associated with something like having a good meal or watching a movie as Hedonic wellbeing; it is the short-term happiness most often associated with having a good time or a moment. Activities such as raising children, volunteering, or pursuing career goals, on the other hand, may not offer pleasure on a day-to-day basis but they provide a sense of fulfilment in the long run.

It is this kind of happiness that researchers define as Eudaimonia and this kind of happiness and well being offer protection from illness, disease, emotional and psychological distress.

These two types of happiness are similar for both men and women, though it has been argued that women are better at differentiating between the two. It is through the Hedonic experience of happiness that the basic differences between male and female happiness exist, but it has been suggested that there are core and controversial issues that impact the happiness of each gender on a more Eudaimonia level as well.

The Gender Dispute of Happiness:

A wealth of research shows the effects of gender on social and motivational behaviours, personality traits, and cognitive performance. The influence of gender roles is different in each society due to their mixed norms, traditions, and belief system. The issue of gender is one of the most complex topics. However, it has the ability for underlying several findings with a research perspective.

According to a new study conducted at the University of Cambridge and the University of Southern California, women report higher levels of unhappiness later in life as compared to men. The research was published in the Journal of Happiness Studies (2008). It is evident that the roles of gender and age on positive psychology constructs of psychological hardiness, emotional quotient, self-efficacy, and happiness. A significant decrease in women's happiness that has been reported over the last 30 years leads researchers to assume that men are happier than women.

<h1 style="text-align:center">Factors that Predict Happiness:</h1>

1. Age: Generally, older people are happier than the younger ones and it is a major factor while measuring happiness. Earlier in life, women are more likely to accomplish their goals (material goals and family life aspirations) than men, thereby increasing their life satisfaction and overall happiness. However, it is later in life that men achieve their goals and are more satisfied with their family life and financial situation and, as a result, their overall happiness surpasses that of women at a later age.

2. Measure: Evaluating happiness is not highly scientific, as happiness is a subjective term, and there's no universal measurement for it. Many studies upon happiness rely on self-assessment. There is evidence to suggest that the reason behind the differences in happiness found between the two genders is due to how they measure their happiness. Women calculate their positive self-esteem based on social and religious associations, whereas men consider their active leisure and mental control for positive self-

esteem. Other assumptions for the difference in men and women's happiness include the theory that women experience more variance or extremes in emotion. Although women are generally happier, it has been observed that women tend to be happier about their love life, family life, and sex life, and changes in these can have a dramatic impact on their level of happiness. Men have been shown to be more affected by their salary, appearance, and physique.

3. Stigma: Due to societal expectations men are less likely to discuss their mental health issues. The society has been following a stigma that a man does not usually go through ill mental health and are mentally strong flatly. Lately, mental health has been openly discussed and many are trying to ignore the prevailing societal norms.

4. Nationality: Lack of opportunities to study, to pursue a particular profession, or lack of freedom and development has been considered as a reason for lower happiness index. Many under-developed nations do not provide a lot of opportunities, leaving the people comparatively less happy.

5. Anger Issues: Anger can break the most beautiful bond with your loved ones. We all have observed that we say or do things when we are angry and regret later. Higher the level of anger and frustration the lower will be the feeling of contentment and bliss.

6. Putting others first: One should know what needs to be prioritized in life. We cannot please everyone and if we keep putting others in the first place all the time we are losing on to what we seek for. Yes, we should not hurt others by our actions but always keeping them as the first priority and ignoring your own self is going to leave us unhappy for the long run.

Earlier studies assumed that women are happier as they consider the emotional and social bond as compared to men who consider the financial status and professional growth above the social bond leading to anger and frustration.

However, recent scientific research has proved that it is not just the social bond and emotional quotient but this is also associated with our brain.

Neuroimaging studies have examined these findings further and concluded that females utilize more areas of the brain containing mirror neurons than males when they assess and process emotions. Mirror neurons allow us to understand the world from other people's perspective, to analyze their actions and intentions. This may explain why women can experience immense joy or deeper sadness.

Psychologically it seems men and women differ in the way they process, assess, and express their emotions. With the exception of anger, women are considered to be vulnerable or intense with their emotions and share it more openly with others. Also, women express more pro-social emotions such as gratitude and empathy which has been linked to greater happiness. This supports the assumption that women's happiness is inter-linked to the relationships than men's.

Yes, women are sensitive to stress, vulnerable to depression, and trauma, but they are also incredibly resilient and significantly more capable of post-traumatic recovery as compared to men. Studies show that this is due to their sociability and ability to connect at a deeper level (emotional level) with others.

Irrespective of the differences between men and women it is important to understand that happiness is not merely the function of individual experience but ripples through social connections. Happiness is infectious and contagious – and it has a positive impact on the health and well-being of everyone.

Earlier, differences in how men and women feel and express emotions were considered solely because of the upbringing and how our parents raising us can reinforce or suppress parts of our basic biology. But now we are aware that the emotional processing in the male and female brain is different. Studies have suggested that our brains have two emotional systems that work simultaneously: the mirror-neuron system, or MNS, and the temporal-parietal junction system, or TPJ. Males seem to use TPJ, and females seem to use MNS more. (Source: The Male Brain, By: By Louann Brizendine, M.D)

We all have said it 'Mom knows it better' and so many times a woman who is close to you tells you beforehand about someone and we later accept it how their gut feeling acted as a guardian angel. Gut feelings are not merely free-floating emotional states but actual physical sensations that convey meaning to certain areas in the brain. Some of this increased gut feeling may have to do with the number of cells available in a woman's brain to trace body sensations which increase after puberty. The increase in estrogens means that girls feel gut sensations and physical pain more than boys do. Some studies speculate that this greater physical sensation in women boosts up the brain's ability to track and feel painful emotions too. The areas of the brain that track gut feelings are larger and highly sensitive in the female brain, according to brain scan studies. Therefore, the relationship between a woman's gut feelings and her instinct is grounded in biology. (Source: The Female Brain, By Louann Brizendine, M.D).

Chapter 3
How to lead a happy life by keeping your Ego aside

We all have been through a stage where we have given importance to someone else more than ourselves; there have also been some phases in life where we have considered our satisfaction as the most important thing. At times when we consider ourselves, without understanding the criticality or the impact of the decision which may lead to disharmony in our relationship with others, is when we are being selfish. However, there's a slight difference between being self- centred and self-care.

When we only care about the good, bad for ourselves without giving due importance to what others may go through is being self-centric, whereas when we do think about what could go wrong without, any hidden motive to hurt someone else's sentiments and giving due importance to your mental peace without ignoring the other person involved is self-care.

You empathize but you don't let your self-respect down is a win-win situation whereas only thinking about oneself and one's esteem, pride leads towards being egoistic and self-centred.

The "I" or self of any person; a person as thinking, feeling, and willing, and differentiating itself from the selves of others and from objects of its thought is usually known as egotism; conceit; self-importance.

According to Freud's psychoanalytic theory, the id is the prime and instinctual part of the mind that contains sexual and aggressive drives and hidden memories, the super-ego operates as a moral conscience, and the ego is the realistic part that lies between the desires of the id and the super-ego.

Ego defense mechanisms are often used by the ego when id behaviour disagrees with reality and either society's morals, norms, and proscription or the individual's expectations as a result of the internalization of these morals, norms, and their prohibitions.

It's very evident and we all have heard and said it many times 'I will be happier if I have a bigger house, a better job, good package, settling down to some desired country' etc., and most of us have achieved almost all the things we have once wished for or aspired for but has the desire to achieve happiness stopped there?

We humans are never satisfied with what we have, because a lot many times the society and the societal norms never let us enjoy what we have and we keep running to achieve more and more until the day we die.

The constant search for happiness in materialistic pleasure is unending and no one knows for how long this will impact our physical and mental well-being.

Usually, when the id and ego are in conflict, that's where the negative impact over one's mental well-being and the conscience get impacted.

There are certain possible ways our ego impacts our mental health and resulting in unhappiness and dissatisfaction:

1.   Self-centred: Most of us just fail to understand the other side of the story. We all have our viewpoint or our look-out based on our experience and we fail empathy. We might be sympathetic towards people but we fail to keep our self in their shoe instead act judgmental and focus on what is better for us. At times this trait is associated with being 'narcissist' where a person tends to care about himself or herself above and beyond any other factor. You tend to ignore the emotional aspect associated and lack empathy.

2.   Self-Depreciation: The act of scolding and berating oneself by belittling, undervaluing, or disparaging oneself or by being excessively modest. We often let ourselves down while going through a rough phase by asking a question to self 'Why me?'; we forget the better opportunities which lie ahead of us and rather than asking 'why me' or 'why not him/her' we need to get back on a track, gather ourselves up and move ahead to

enhance our skill sets and achieve what's worth the time and effort. It is not easy to ignore the pain (emotional, physical, or any other mishap) but you can always consider one small downfall as a baby step towards your betterment which we usually fail to realize.

3.   The Revenge Tactic or Tit for Tat: As they say 'what goes around, comes around' and 'every action has an equal and opposite reaction' but doing that with an intention to hurt someone just because you were hurt is unethical. But we all wished for that at least once. When we had a break-up or when the less deserving candidate got the promotion and you were not considered irrespective of being the star employee or whatsoever may be the reason. Having the tendency to hurt others intentionally just because their actions have hurt you will leave you in despair dragging us towards negativity.

4.   Impulsive Behaviour: We usually have 3-5 seconds to react or to respond towards something. It could be a situation like a mishap, a conversation, or anything else. The sooner we

realize the better it is. A very common incident we all have come across somehow when we are out with friends, enjoying a few drinks, and the next morning you wake up to texts from an ex? Your immediate reaction is of regret, self-deprecation followed by damage control. How about the test you opted to cheat on in school that resulted in a much worse grade than if you had made the attempt without preparation? Or the presentation you copied because you didn't do your due diligence on the front end and it resulted in a demotion or bad remark at work? Either of the situation, where if you would have acted more rationally than being impulsive or impatient so you wouldn't have repented later; but we usually underestimate the importance of those 3-5 seconds and ended up into a never-ending loop of our impulsive behaviour and regret if something goes wrong.

5.   Anger: The reaction which breaks a lot of relation. When anger and ego meet, grudges and hostility enter. We let our anger to sculpt our newly revamped ego and see everything bad in life as warranted and every day as the prospect

for something bad. As we adopt the 'shit happens' outlook, our perception dwindles and we see ourselves as less deserving of blame and we keep blaming the external factors for all the happenings rather than owning up to what we have done.

What can help us fix it?

We need to keep our ego aside to understand what really matters. It's not always what is good for us but what is also good for the people associated with us, what can help towards self-betterment.

1. You attract what you seek: Do things which give you pleasure and satisfaction and help you to fulfil your emotional well-being too. Stop self-doubting and comparing and remember no one else knows you better than you.

2. Connect with others on a deeper level: Empathise with people, listen more than just hearing. Give due respect to the bond you share with them.

3. Take a leap of faith: When in doubt, try to take a break but remember everything has a risk factor associated with it and you need to stop self-doubting and take that leap of faith while doing something which really matters to you.

4. Don't let the societal norms define you: You know yourself better than anyone else. Make sure if you want to do something it's entirely what you want to do to attain the self-satisfaction and not something to please someone.

A very important factor which has impacted our lives lately is the 'virtual world'. With the advancement in technology and globalisation, we are able to connect the world at one platform just by one click, but everything has its perks and perils. Technology has surely made things easier but it has also made humans lazy. Likewise, the 'virtual world or social media' has brought people staying in different corners of the world together but has also affected the real social relations greatly.

"A recent study from the University of Pennsylvania suggests our virtual social networks can have an adverse effect. According to researchers at UPenn, through experimental data and self-monitoring, this study is the first to show a causal link that an increase in social media use can decrease well-being.

When we spend hours on apps, such as Facebook, Instagram and Snapchat, passively scrolling through our feeds and negatively comparing ourselves to "one-sided" views of other people's lives, we are doing serious harm to our mental well-being. The fear of missing out (FOMO), which means, witnessing people in your network having a good time without you, also contributes to negative feelings.

So that whole fear of missing out in which people get very anxious about other people having connections, friendships and relationships, that they aren't a part of, is another aspect of the problem. When you use too much social media, you feel like your own life doesn't measure up to the virtual status and you constantly feel that you are not always invited to things that everyone else is invited to.

Studies have shown when there is an increase in digital media, especially for young people; there is a decline in sleep, exercise, social interactions and attending religious services compared to those who do not spend so much time in virtual reality which impacts the mental health adversely.

On contrary in a study, "The Social Media Party: Fear of Missing Out (FOMO), Social Media Intensity, Connection, and Well-Being," the researchers focused on the effect FOMO has on social media use, social connections to others and psychological well-being.

The study, which was conducted by James A. Roberts, Ph.D., The Ben H. Williams Professor of Marketing, and Meredith David, Ph.D., assistant professor of marketing in Baylor's Hankamer School of Business, was published in the International Journal of Human-Computer Interaction.

According to Roberts, approximately 75% of young adults may struggle with some level of FOMO.

"The human need to belong is an innate drive that dictates much of our behavior," said Roberts via a statement. "Social media capitalizes on this need to belong. Social media has a dual nature. It lets us interact with others, which is good, but it also exposes us to more social opportunities than we can take part in and that fosters a sense of missing out and inadequacy."

Another problem with social media the study found, was that it is often used passively – in what it has been described as "creeping on people", cyber bullying, or "viewing pages without interacting (stalking)" and such activity leads to overall decreased levels of happiness. Creeping does not foster social connections.

But the general FOMO can in fact, lead to happier people if it also drives those individuals to use social media to make meaningful connections.

The Type of Engagement Is What Matters

Using or not using social media may not be the point, but rather how one uses it.

Social media is likely to have different implications on happiness or wellbeing depending on the type of social media engagement activity, as well as the characteristics of the person using the social media, and the time of social media usage.

Feeling connected to others, gathering useful information, providing or seeking advice or volunteer activities may be important aspects of happiness that can be inflated by social media use. Overuse of social media resulting in sleep deprivation or social avoidance can be detrimental to wellbeing, some people who are very reactive to fear of missing out or social jealousy may also experience negative impacts on mood from social media use."

It's not totally right to say that the virtual world is the sole aspect which affects the mental well-being and creating a hindrance to one's happiness, but it would be absolutely wrong to assume the 'virtual world' to be the only reality.

Important Note

It's important that you spend a minimum of 10 minutes a day thinking of all good things and implement positive change in you because it is you who can lead yourself towards the path of happiness and to generate the zeal or willingness to be happy.

The moment you cannot control your feelings and emotions, you are letting someone else have that power on you and they direct you to act accordingly. It is as similar as sharing your laptop's password with people and letting them misuse your personal or work data by accessing it. Here you are letting someone else manipulate your thoughts and your emotions, which shouldn't be allowed, may it be anybody.

Chapter 4

Work - Life & Mental Health

Work-life balance and mental well-being or mental health is a topic being discussed over a decade now and with the change in the environment and the working pattern, a lot is still being discussed.

Approximately 264 million people suffer from depression globally, which is considered to be one of the main causes of disability, with several others suffering from anxiety or symptoms of anxiety. The WHO conducted a study that estimated that depression and anxiety disorders cost US$ 1 trillion every year due to a downfall in productivity globally. Unemployment is also a potential factor for mental health problems

For over a decade the discussion on how a negative work environment can impact one's mental health and personal life is ongoing. This was also the theme of World Mental Health Day 2017 by the World Federation for Mental Health (WFMH) on their Sliver Jubilee

(25th Anniversary) where the topic was discussed how adversely the unfavourable work environment can impact one's mental health.

Sound mental health enables people to realize their potential, helps in coping with the normal stresses of life, work proactively, and contributes to their organization. However, the increasing burden of mental illness is alarming. Globally, one-in-four people are likely to experience a mental health issue at some point in their lives. An estimation of over 300 million people to suffer from depression, approximately 4.4% of the world's population and somewhere around 800,000 people take their own lives every year.

"Mental health-promoting actions and strategies are oriented to upliftment, choice, association, and involvement. They strengthen protective aspects, reduce risk factors, and build on the social aspects of health, often providing partnerships across sectors.

With so many of us juggling between heavy workloads, managing relationships, family responsibilities, and squeezing in outside interests it shouldn't be a shock when the global organizations showcase the numbers like 1 out of 4 individuals are expected to face the mental stress and it is absolutely not healthy nor balanced.

Extreme stress also weakens our immune systems and makes us prone to various ailments from colds to backaches or heart disease. The newest research shows that chronic stresses can potentially double one's risk of having a heart attack

While we all need a certain level of stress to spur us on and to help us perform at our best, the key to handle and manage stress lies in that one magic word: balance. Not only achieving a healthy work-life balance as an attainable goal but also workers and businesses witness the rewards. When workers are balanced and happy, they are more productive, reduce absenteeism, and are more likely to continue in their jobs.

Many studies and researchers have proved that one's happiness can be influenced by expressing gratitude, nurturing relationships, physical exercise, or spiritual activities.

Work-related risk factors for health:

There are many factors that impact mental health in the workplace. Major factor relates to the interactions between types of work, the organizational and managerial environment, the skills and competencies of employees, and the support provided to the employees to perform their work some of the factors are mentioned below:

• inappropriate health and safety policies;

• lack of communication and management practices;

• restricted participation in decision-making or decentralization of power over one's area of work;

• lower levels of support and lack of appreciation for employees;

• income disparity;

• gender role biases and inequality;

• improper working hours;

• Unclear tasks, targets, or organizational objectives.

Factors associated with risk for mental health may also be related to the job description, such as unsuitable tasks for the person's competencies, or a high and unrelenting workload. Some jobs may carry a potential higher personal risk than others (e.g. first responders and humanitarian workers), which can impact one's mental health and be a cause of symptoms of mental disorders, or lead to harmful consumption of alcohol or psychoactive drugs. The risk usually increased in situations where there is a lack of team cohesion, harmony, or social support.

Bullying and psychological harassment (also known as "mobbing") are often reported causes of work-related stress by workers and create risks to the health of employee/s. They are associated with both psychological and physical issues. These adverse health consequences also cost for employers in terms of reduced productivity and increased staff absenteeism and turnover, further having a negative impact on family and social interactions for a longer run.

Initial Triggers associated With Mental Health:

Experiencing one or more of the following feelings or behaviours can be a red flag or a trigger for the initial stage of the mental health issue:

- Eating or sleeping too much or too little.
- Avoiding social gatherings, meeting people and usual activities.
- Having low or no energy.
- Feeling numb.
- Having unexplained aches and pains majors the psychological heaviness.
- Feeling helpless and disappointed.
- Excessive use of alcohol and drugs.
- Frequent mood swings.
- Furious and reactive, easily getting provoked.
- Over thinking and over analysing.
- Lack of rationale and high importance to assumptions.
- Constant thoughts about self-harming.
- Feeling exhausted and inability to perform day-to-day tasks.

Creating a healthy workplace

An important component of attaining a healthy work environment is the initiation of governmental legislation, strategies, and policies as emphasized by the European Union Compass contribution to this area. One can consider a workplace to be sound and safe only where workers and managers actively participate in the working environment by enhancing and safeguarding the health, safety, and mental well-being of all human assets. In 2014 an academic report suggested that interventions should take a 3-pronged approach:

• Safeguarding mental and emotional health by reducing work-related risk elements.

• Encourage mental well-being by developing the positive facet of work and the strengths of employees.

• Giving due consideration and importance to mental health problems regardless of cause.

Building on this, a guide from the World Economic Forum highlights steps organizations can initiate to implement a healthy workplace, including:

• Understanding the workplace settings and how they can be adapted to execute better mental health for different employees.

• Execution and getting motivated by the people in the organization who have implemented such plans into actions.

• Learning and implementing what other companies, who have taken action, done.

• The mindset of many strategical levels in the organization is 'we always have an alternative of X employee in the market' needs to be changed. It's high time that the importance of an individual employee is given due importance in helping to develop better policies for workplace mental health.

• Accessibility of sources of support and where people can find help should be given due importance.

Creativity and good practices that protect and promote mental wellbeing in the workplace include:

• Execution and application of health and safety policies and practices, along with identification of distress, hazardous use of psychoactive substances and illness and providing resources to handle them;

• Letting the staffs know that support is available;

• Encouraging employees participation in decision-making, conveying a feeling of belongingness and participation; organizational practices that support a healthy work-life balance;

• Scope for the career development of employees; and

• Recognizing and rewarding the contribution which makes the employees motivated and valued at work.

Despite the rules laid by the International and Local bodies, the increase in the issues relating to mental wellbeing and work-life are still been observed. Long hours at work, unequal pay or favoritism during promotion, rotational shifts, and odd hours of work have adverse impact the physical and mental health of the individuals and very less has been focused by the organizations in general.

A lot of mental health issues arise due to the above-mentioned work-life impact on personal life, as many have been unable to spend due time with family and friends which leads to frustration and dissatisfaction towards one's work and working pattern.

It is preferred to have a defined routine so that you are able to manage your life at work and a life outside work, as the social relationship you hold is equally important as your organizational relationship.

Self-reported happiness relates strongly to:

Self-reported happiness relates strongly to:

• Activities of dopamine or the brain's pleasure centre.

• Well-being, positive emotional arousal, and future intentions.

Brain Responses in Two Pictures (MRI Scans)

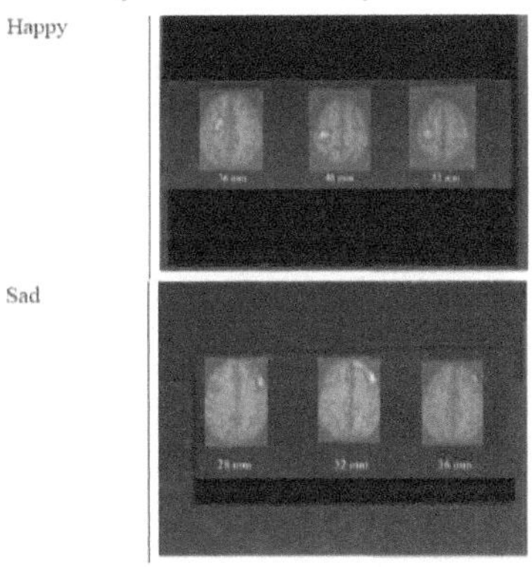

Source: Richard Davidson, University of Wisconsin

Reported happiness is correlated with...

• individual's evaluation of happiness by social relationships.

• individual's evaluation of happiness by a partner or a spouse.

• Recalling the good and bad events.

• The response to stress via heart rate and blood pressure.

• if the person is prone to coronary heart disease.

The concept higher the income results into increasing the level of happiness is now not correlated ("Easterlin Paradox").

There have been shreds of evidence of genuine work-life balance issues in modern society. It is important that policies in the coming years need to concentrate on non-materialistic aspects. One can keep writing or discussing about the reasons and symptoms of 'mental health' at work & how it impacts the personal life but it is highly important that we come out of the stigma we as a society have created and discuss it as openly as we can discuss about our physical health.

Chapter 5

Conclusion

Happiness is a State of Mind

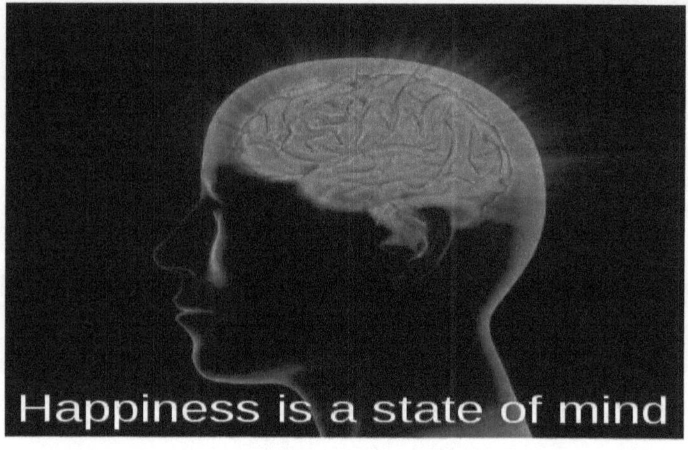

Three simple steps will definitely make difference in your life

1. Unloading the thought which makes you unhappy: So how you will unload your thoughts? Yes, the best way to unload your thoughts is to writing dairy of writing in any sheet of paper if you don't want to share with your friends of anyone else.

2. List the things which makes you happy: Among the list select the one and concentrate on it develop career on it or improvise it which makes your journey happy.

3. If you're stuck in taking decision: Then write it is a paper and address to universe in some time you'll definitely get a solution.

While sleeping and when you wake up say at least 10 times "I will be happy and healthy all the time"

Book gives suggestion on the basis of interview with psychology expert, academicians, journalist, motivational leader, scientific research and self-experience.

The only thumb rule to change yourself is willingness to change. Making small changes in life style bring huge difference in body and mind.

To fill any positive things you should first remove negative things. Negative things are self-created or created by observation.

When you are sleeping remember good things happened in that day instead thinking what went wrong. Similarly, when you wake up show gratitude for whatever good has happened in life.

When you wake up repeat 10 times which will be recorded by your brain. You can just say "Be happy and be Healthy"

Look at the mirror and smile that gives you energy and confidence.

12 Ways to Unlock Your Inner Happiness during Holiday

The holidays are just around the corner. You are running around for everyone else, having trouble saying no to your commitments, and your energy has already depleted. Before you realize it, you have put the relationship you have with yourself, your most important relationship on the back burner. The holidays are a time to decompress, re-evaluate where you are in life, and cultivate your inner happiness.

1. **Don't compare yourself to others.**

Your life is unique, so don't measure your own worth by comparing yourself to those around you. Even regarding yourself as better than your peers is detrimental to your happiness, as you're fostering judgmental feelings towards others and an unhealthy sense of superiority. Measure your own success based on your progress alone, not that of others. Engaging in upward and downward social comparison on either end of the spectrum is not an option to enhance your self-esteem, because it will backfire on you.

2. **Surround yourself with positive people.**

The saying "misery loves company" is entirely trite, but nonetheless true. That's why you need to choose friends who are optimistic and happy themselves, as you will be surrounded with positive energy. It is this type of energy that will bounce directly off of you. Toxic negative people will leave you feeling drained and hollow, and physically/emotionally/mentally unable to move. These people are called emotional vampires, so try to steer clear of them, or if that's not a realistic option at least limit your interactions with them if you can.

3. Realize that you don't need others' approval.

It's important to follow your own dreams and desires without letting naysayers stand in your way. It's fine to seek others' opinions and advice but happy people stay true to their own hearts and don't get bogged down with the need for outside approval. People pleasing can take a toll on one's health and sanity, so refrain from engaging in that empty pursuit.

4. Take time to truly listen.

Active listening helps you soak in the wisdom of others and allows you to quiet your own mind at the same time. Intense listening can help you feel content while helping you gain different perspectives. Practice the art of listening well, and resist the urge to chime in while they talk in order to say what you want to say.

5. Nurture social relationships.

Positive *personal* social relationships are a key to happiness, so be sure you make time to visit with friends, family and your significant other. This means connecting in person, face to face, not via social network or other social media platforms, which has become quite the norm these days.

6. Yoga

Research shows that yoga helps you keep your mind focused, calms your nerves and supports inner peace shows it can even lead to epigenetic/physical changes in your brain that actually makes you happier.

7. Eat well.

What you eat directly impacts your mood and energy levels in both the short and long term. Whereas eating right can prime your body and brain to be in a focused, happy state, eating processed junk foods will leave you sluggish and prone to chronic disease. Learn to eat the right foods both for physical and emotional wellness. You cannot be truly healthy until you have the right balanced components in play.

8. Physical Exercise

Exercise boosts levels of health-promoting brain chemicals like serotonin, dopamine, and norepinephrine, which may help buffer some of the effects of stress and also relieve some symptoms of depression. Rather than viewing exercise as a medical tool to lose weight, prevent disease, and ultimately live longer – granted all amazing benefits that will occur in the future – try viewing exercise as a daily tool to immediately enhance your frame of mind, reduce stress and feel overall happier.

9. Live minimally.

Clutter has a way of sucking the energy right out of you and replacing it with feelings of chaos. Clutter is an often-unrecognized and unconscious source of stress that prompts feelings of anxiety, frustration, distraction and even guilt, so give your home and office a clutter makeover, purging it of the excess papers, files, knick knacks and other "stuff" that not only takes up space in your physical environment, but also in your mind. The messy outside often times reflects what is going on the inside.

10. Be honest.

Every time you refrain from telling the truth, your stress levels are likely to increase and your self-esteem will crumble/plummet just a little bit more. Plus, if others find out you're a liar it will damage your personal and professional relationships. Telling the truth, on the other hand, boosts your mental health and allows others to build trust in you.

11. Establish personal control.

Avoid letting other people dictate the way you live. Instead, establish personal control in your life that allows you to fulfil your own goals and dreams, as well as a great sense of personal self-worth. Your self-control is your dignity. Refrain from giving others power in a variety of ways.

12. **Accept what cannot be changed.**

Everything in your life is not going to be perfect, and that's perfectly all right. Happy people learn to accept injustices and setbacks in their life that they cannot change, and do not become embittered by their experiences. Instead, they put their energy on changing what they can control for the better to live a happier and more meaningful life.

So, although our life circumstances can certainly after our happiness in the short run, much of our happiness in the long run is surprisingly independent of what happens to us. More than we wish to admit, happiness is at least as much a function of what we make of our lives as our lives themselves.

We decided to gather a primary source of identifying what can actually help us to walk towards the path which is filled with inner peace and happiness.

We contacted 7 people working in different field to share their thoughts over 5 open ended questions which is actually the summarization of all the topics we tried to cover in our book.

We are providing you with the crux of the answers received for each question answered by our experts:

Que 1. How would you like to define happiness?

To our surprise all of our experts were with an opinion that the term 'happiness' is very subjective and may hold different meaning for different individual.

However, the agreed on a point where all of them believe that it is an inner feeling which one experience after doing or achieving something which provides a self-satisfaction.

Que 2. Do you think the virtual world has mislead the meaning of happiness?

A mixed response was received for this question as the experts do believe that people get influenced easily by others and it does impact them adversely but on contrary the virtual world has given fairly wide opportunities to showcase one's skills or talent.

It is important to understand that not everything on the social media is true and one should be cautious about surfing and sharing details over virtual world. As fancy and great platform to connect with people across the globe there has also been an increase in cases of cyber bullying, insomnia, anxiety and depression among youth as they tend to compare their lives with someone they don't know and get impacted negatively.

In the virtual space we are actually loosing on to the real relationship we share with our friends, family members and sooner or later with our kids too.

Que 3. Does materialistic pleasure defines happiness?

It was a matter of a little amusement when few of our experts accepted the fact that 'yes materialistic pleasure provide happiness' (does not defines happiness) but the happiness achieved from them are short lived.

"Someone once said, materialism is important, because it's far better to cry on your yacht than on your bicycle." It is surely important to gain such materialistic possession to survive in the world but completely relying on them is surely not a wise thing.

However, all the experts do agree that the happiness achieved through such materials are short lived and often doesn't last at all.

Most of us spend a lifetime just working so we can buy all the materialistic pleasure that catches our fancy and we end up losing focus of why we started on our journey in the first place, while materialist wealth definitely cannot be completely abolished, it's important to not become dependent on it.

Que 4. Do you think 'Ego acts as a hindrance' whereas, 'Empathy acts as a path towards happiness'?

Ego does acts as a hindrance but it also leads to the bottom of our own.

It is important to understand the Id and Super Ego which dominates the 'I, Me, Myself' part while ego can be a positive reinforcement to know oneself better. A channelized ego can help you achieve a better side however, a conflict between the id and conscience can lead to the disastrous impact of an ego over any relationship creating chaos and frustration acting as a hindrance towards happiness.

Whereas, Empathy always acts as a path towards happiness. Understand feeling of others always gives inner happiness to both parties. It is a win-win situation where you help your inner self understand you better and while you put yourself in someone else's shoes helps you to understand the emotional chaos the other person is going through. You tend to analyse the situation better and respond positively when you empathize.

Que 5. How to remove negative thoughts?

There are so many ways to overcome negative thoughts and we hope few of the best practises our experts recommend can be helpful for our readers:

- Listening to Music: Music has been the best treatment for your mood. Music therapy act as a miracle on one's thought process and it is also a proven fact that good music reduces stress.

- Spending time with the loved one's: May it be your parents, siblings or close friends spending time with a good companion is the best way to reduce your negative thoughts and get out of stress.

- Spending less time on Social Media: Though studies have suggested that avoiding social media may or may not have any behavioural change but taking a break for a while is surely not a bad idea. Maybe you built up a new hobby to spare your time on.

- Focusing on the small goals: It is important to focus on small goals to accomplish and to feel motivated to work towards a bigger goal. This helps us to ensure that we give due importance to little things in life and while there are negative thoughts over ruling our mind such small achievements will help us feel positive and to work towards our bigger goal with more zeal and positivity. Also, at times the problems we are facing is due to external factors and its beyond our control in a situation like this one should not let it impact the mind so much as its not in one's hand and it's better to focus on what can be done rather than crying over external factors.

- Do things that makes you happy: Dancing, painting, reading or spending some time working out or anything that gives you happiness or makes you feel content can be practised while overcoming negative thoughts.
- Spending time with kids and pets: Kids and pets have a different level of energy and the selfless love they hold for people they are close with. Spending time with them can act as a quick stress buster.

There are few other ways too which can help you overcome the negative thoughts:

a. Hugging a Tree: Sounds funny or weird?

According to the book Blinded by Science by Matthew Silverstone, there is evidence that trees provide health benefits for mental illnesses such as Attention Deficit Hyperactivity Disorder and depression. Children function better cognitively and emotionally when they interact with plants. Although many believe it's the green open spaces that contribute to the effect, Silverstone demonstrates that the vibrational properties of trees and plants offer health benefits. An article in Natural News indicates that if you drink a glass of water that has been treated with a 10HZ vibration, your blood coagulation rates will change immediately on ingesting the treated water. Hugging a tree increases levels of hormone oxytocin. This hormone is responsible for feeling calm and emotional bonding. When hugging a tree, the hormones serotonin and dopamine make you feel happier. It is important to use this "free" space of a forest we were given by nature to holistically heal ourselves.

b. Relationships are essential: A major study followed hundreds of men for more than 70 years, and found the happiest (and healthiest) were those who cultivated strong relationships with people they trusted to support them. (Source: The Harvard Study of Adult Development)

c. Time beats money: A number of studies have shown that happier people prefer to have more time in their lives than more money. Even trying to approach life from that mind-set seems to make people more content. (Source: Business Insider)

d. But it helps to have enough money to pay the bills: People's well-being rises along with income levels up to an annual salary of about $75,000, studies have found. (That number probably varies depending on your cost of living, however.) (Source: Proceedings of the National Academy of Sciences)

e. It's worth stopping to smell the roses: People who slow down to reflect on good things in their lives report being more satisfied. Appreciate the little things and small achievements in life. (Source: Journal of Personality and Social Psychology)

f. Fun is more valuable than material items: People tend to be happier if they spend their money on experiences instead of things. Researchers have also found that buying things that allow you to have experiences — like rock climbing shoes or a new book to read — can also increase happiness. (Sources: Psychological Science, Journal of Consumer Psychology)

g. Acts of kindness boost the mood: Give your friends a ride to the airport or spend an afternoon volunteering. Some research has shown that people who perform such acts report being happier. (Source: Review of General Psychology)

h. Meditation: If we have control on over emotion then definitely we can achieve what ever we want and stay happy. To have emotional control and raise our inner strength meditation is every much necessary. Meditation is less about faith and more about altering consciousness, finding awareness, and achieving peace.

There are three popular types of meditation practice:

- mindfulness meditation

- spiritual meditation

- focused meditation

a. Mindfulness Meditation

Mindfulness meditation originates from Buddhist teachings and is the most popular meditation technique in the West.

In mindfulness meditation, you pay attention to your thoughts as they pass through your mind. You don't judge the thoughts or become involved with them. You simply observe and take note of any patterns. This practice combines concentration with awareness. You may find it helpful to focus on an object or your breath while you observe any bodily sensations, thoughts, or feelings. This type of meditation is good for people who don't have a teacher to guide them, as it can be easily practiced alone.

b. Spiritual Meditation:

Spiritual meditation is used in Eastern religions, such as Hinduism and Daoism, and in Christian faith. It's similar to prayer in that you reflect on the silence around you and seek a deeper connection with your God or Universe

c. Focused Meditation:

Focused meditation involves concentration using any of the five senses. For example, you can focus on something internal, like your breath, or you can bring in external influences to help focus your attention. Try counting mala beads, listening to a gong, or staring at a candle flame.

This practice may be simple in theory, but it can be difficult for beginners to hold their focus for longer than a few minutes at first. If your mind does wander, it's important to come back to the practice and refocus.

As the name suggests, this practice is ideal for anyone who requires additional focus in their life.

How to get started?

The easiest way to begin is to sit quietly and focus on your breath.

"Sit consistently for 20 minutes a day and do this for 100 days straight," recommends Pedram Shojai, author of "The Urban Monk" and founder of Well.org. "Couple that with an additional 2 to 5 minutes of meditation throughout the day to break up the chaos, and you will soon be feeling the benefits."

There is much evidence trusted source supporting the numerous benefits of meditation.

Meditation can help:

- lower blood pressure
- reduce anxiety
- decrease pain
- ease symptoms of depression
- improve sleep

We have mentioned it in the very beginning as there is no thumb rule to define happiness but there is a path that leads you towards it.

Clicking pictures and showing the world that you are happy is not what the real happiness is, it is more apt when you have at least one person to share it with. It's very important that we need to stay content and give due importance to the people in and around us rather than just being focused on what happens on the virtual world. Let that not define you. Let no societal norms define happiness for you it is you who knows what you want and what is that can help you attain a better mental and emotional health.

Talk to people when you need them and reciprocate the same when they need you. In the world where you can be anything be a little kind to yourself and with others. The door is never closed forever you either find a key to open it or else you knock it so that someone staying inside can open it for you and guide you through the path which leads you towards 'Happiness'.

Now since you have knocked the door of happiness, we hope your journey be filled with happiness and contentment.